SILVER IMAGE

Early British Photography

Cv/Visual Arts Research Volume 68

Silver Image
Early British Photography

ISBN 1-904727-63-8
ISSN 1476-9980

This interview was first published in
Cv Journal of the Arts
(London: The Artist's Journal Ltd 1989)

British Library Cataloguing in Publication Data.
A catalogue record of this book is available from the British Library

A digital format publication produced by
Cv Publications, Barley Mow Business Centre,
Barley Mow Passage, London W4 4PH
www.tracksdirectory.ision.co.uk

Cv/VAR Interview
The transcript of the original recording was checked, amended and approved by the featured subject for publication.

Cv/Visual Arts Research

The survey began in April 1988 as interviews with jewellers, fashion designers and furniture restorers, based at Old Loom House in Whitechapel, launching a quarterly review *Cv Journal of Art and Crafts*. *Cv Journal* was published to 1992 and the collection of interviews, features and reviews provided the foundation of the Cv/Visual Arts Research archive and subsequent publications. Following *Cv Journal* the data-base shifted towards electronic publishing, allowing a greater flexibility of communication.

Cv/*VAR* addresses the fields of academic research, galleries and museums worldwide, and a non-specialist readership. In this respect the archive has been re-organised as a file system which may be accessed as individual articles or collated volumes, according to specific requirements. The data base is categorized as *Interviews-Artists; Curators and Collections; CraftsDirectory; Small Histories; Social Studies and Studio Work.* Titles are published as conventional books and information files made by digital process as print on demand, as well as CDs and DVDs in Cv Publications' software catalogue. There are now over ninety titles published in the series.

Contents

SILVER IMAGE

The Collection of The Royal Photographic Society Bath
Interview with Curator Pamela Roberts, recorded 27.10.93

Cv/VAR. Who started the Royal Photographic Society, and was its motivating force?

PR. It was formed in 1853, as an offshoot of the Royal Society of Arts. The motivating force was Roger Fenton, who was the first secretary of the society and his work is one of our biggest collections of photography, we have about seven hundred and fifty photographs in all. Fenton had been over to Paris, he'd worked there with photographers such as Gustave Le Gray and Henri Le Secq.

SILVER IMAGE

EARLY BRITISH PHOTOGRAPHY

In 1882 they set up Le Societé Héliographique, and he was impressed by the fact that there was a separate photographic society, so, he came back and set up a similar sort of thing in the UK. It was also stimulated by The Great Exhibition at The Crystal Palace in London 1851, where photography was shown en masse for the first time. There was also a large photographic exhibition held at the Royal Society of Arts at the end of 1852, and from the interest generated, Fenton called a meeting of like-minded individuals, to form a Photographic Society.

SILVER IMAGE

EARLY BRITISH PHOTOGRAPHY

Did they have any stated ideals or agenda?

Their ideals were to advance the art and science of photography *(reads)* 'The object of the Photographic Society is the promotion of the Art and Science of Photography by the interchange of thought and experience among Photographers, and it is hoped this object may, to some considerable extent, be effected by the periodical meetings of the Society.' At the first meeting it was decided they would establish a photographic journal. The first issue was in March 1853, and is still being published. They would have annual exhibitions of work of their members and establish a darkroom

SILVER IMAGE

EARLY BRITISH PHOTOGRAPHY

in London. The first base they had was in Russell Square.

What was their funding?

They weren't funded and never have been. This is one of the problems of the RPS. Fenton was a friend of Prince Albert, who was very interested in photography and had a darkroom at Windsor Castle. Fenton had worked with Prince Albert prior to 1853, on things like Adult Education Classes; like the Working Men's Association in Camden Town. This was set up to assist working men's appreciation of the arts; stonemasonry, crafts, and so on. Albert was very interested in these philanthropic,

SILVER IMAGE

EARLY BRITISH PHOTOGRAPHY

educational projects, and he and Queen Victoria were the Society's first Patrons. He came to all the meetings and was really quite involved. However we did not get the Royal addition to our title until 1894.

Has the RPS always been in Bath?

No, we moved here in 1979. The society moved around London and gradually acquired bigger and bigger premises as the Collection grew; first in Russell Square and then at Prince's Gate, Kensington, in the 1960s and '70s. That building was sold to the Iranian Embassy, the one which was later stormed by the SAS. When the lease was up for

SILVER IMAGE

EARLY BRITISH PHOTOGRAPHY

renewal at the South Audley Street site at Hyde Park, they decided to form a National Centre for Photography, with a study centre based on our own Collection, which is phenomenal. At that point they decided to move out of London to Bath, and opened here in 1980.

In the early days of the RPS the members were the experimenters with the medium. They were scientists and artists, a lot of them had an artistic background. Fenton was a painter, Rejlander as well, and many of them earned their living as artists. The society was seen as a meeting place for new inventions the idea was to bring in your research , say, having reached a certain stage with a coated glass negative, but with something not quite right, and people could contribute to it. It was like a think tank. All the cameras were pretty big, compared with what we've got now. Fenton had a photographic van converted from an old vintner's carriage, which he stripped out and painted white to reflect the heat of the Crimea. It was kitted out internally as a darkroom. Fenton worked with 20″ x 16″ glass negatives, which slid into the back of a camera with a 22″ x 18″ span. So he worked with a huge camera to achieve a great depth of field.

SILVER IMAGE

EARLY BRITISH PHOTOGRAPHY

At the Victoria and Albert Museum they have the four feet square negatives in their collection, dating from the late 1850s. These were sheets of glass which had to be hand coated just before exposure. It wasn't something that could be done back in your own darkroom, you had to take them onto the field. There are letters from Fenton in the Crimea describing how they had to be out by seven in the morning. After that the light became too strong and it was phenomenally hot. They were working in temperatures of 110 degrees, plus there was the dust. You coated your negative with collodion, which is a very sticky mixture, like nail varnish,

SILVER IMAGE

EARLY BRITISH PHOTOGRAPHY

Agnew's in London, to go out on their behalf and photograph the campaign, and to bring the prints back, which were then sold in sets; either mounted in albums, or sold as loose prints. Agnew's wanted a variety of formats at a variety of prices, so they could sell as many as they could.

The pioneer of photography, Henry Fox Talbot, was based near Bath at Lacock Abbey, and the RPS has a major holding of his works. Did he use glass negatives too?

No, this was before glass came in. He worked with paper negatives. Nicephore Niepce had invented Heliogravure, which was an image etched on a pewter plate. He then worked with Louis-Jaques Mande, to develop what became the Daguerrotype. Niepce died and Daguerre took over, some would say, taking all the credit as well. Daguerre and Niepce invented a unique image, if you wanted another Daguerreotype of yourself, you had to go back to the studio and sit again. Fox Talbot invented the negative, from which you can get an infinite number of positives. That was made on paper, and therefore you got the grain of the paper coming through. The image was saturated into the paper. Talbot started by coating the paper with a light sensitive solution putting a leaf on, a piece of

SILVER IMAGE

EARLY BRITISH PHOTOGRAPHY

lace, or something that sunlight could pass through, exposing it. But the light sensitive solution would darken, which was a problem. What Talbot discovered, with a lot of help from John Herschel, was how to fix it. That was the important thing; that he had control of the darkening action. From that stage you could then take your paper negative, wax it to make it more translucent, then sandwich it with another piece of coated paper put the two together in a printing frame out in the sun, and in that way you got your positive image.

People had to sit rigidly still for several minutes for a portrait?

SILVER IMAGE

EARLY BRITISH PHOTOGRAPHY

Yes. Initially his exposure times were very long, but as he found out more about solutions, he could make more rapidly reacting mixtures. Then there were better lenses. His first cameras were tiny little mousehole contraptions, which eventually progressed to bigger cameras, longer focal lengths, and more rapid exposures.

And what about the Hill and Adamson photographs ?

They were slightly later. Talbot put a patent on his invention, and thereafter, everybody who wanted to use it in a professional way had to pay him rather large amounts of money. But that didn't apply to amateurs, nor did it apply in Scotland. Hill and Adamson were based in Edinburgh. David Octavius Hill was a painter, the brothers John and Robert Adamson were both chemists, but Robert got together with David Octavius Hill, who wanted to use photographs as an aide-memoire for his painting a large tableau of the Free Presbytarian Meeting in Scotland, that contained some five hundred people. He thought if he could get them all in individual groups, he could record each one for the painted portrait. Hill, therefore, would do the composition, the lighting and the dramatic effect, and Adamson would do the chemical side of it. What happened

SILVER IMAGE

EARLY BRITISH PHOTOGRAPHY

was that Hill became more obsessed with the photography side of it than the painting. After they'd recorded a lot of groups, they started the first real documentary exploration They had plans to go round Scotland to record the life of the villages. They went to Newhaven and photographed the fishing community there, which is the most wonderful series. We have about four hundred Hill and Adamsons here. They were going to go to the Highlands and Lowlands, and document the various ways of life, when Adamson died at an early age, possibly brought on by the chemicals he used. He was slightly tubercular, but the horrible stuff he

SILVER IMAGE

EARLY BRITISH PHOTOGRAPHY

worked with didn't help, such as potassium cyanide. Hill's subsequent partnerships never gelled in the same way.

Were these early experiments preserved by the photographers' families, and in what state did they come to you?

Yes, by and large. The chemical state is amazingly good. To go back to Prince Albert; he started collecting photographs to chart its progress over fourteen years. If you go through our minute books for the 1850s, Gustave Le Gray brought over some of his seascapes and left them in London, though they later disappeared, as we don't have them any

SILVER IMAGE

EARLY BRITISH PHOTOGRAPHY

more. By 1923 the new president of the society, John Dudley Johnston decided he would give a speech about the society's famous past, and the photographers who had been involved. Johnston went to the archives, such as they were, to look at what was there, and all there was were a hundred framed pictures from a variety of people, that had been presented to the society. So he decided he would start avidly collecting photographs, forming what is probably the first collection of photography in the world. He also started researching the past history, going to the descendants of the photographers, who were not far enough removed to have split the collections. So at this point, all Fenton's material came in, over the next ten years. Also the Julia Margaret Cameron collection, of about seven hundred and eighty photographs. Regarding Fox Talbot, in 1935 his last living descendant Matilda Fox Talbot, who was unmarried, with no children to pass the collection on to, gave Lacock, the abbey and the whole village, to the National Trust. However, she decided to give some of the photographs to the two big collections, the RPS and the Science Museum. Humphrey Barclay, who was the curator at the Science Museum, and Dudley Johnston, were invited to Lacock to help

SILVER IMAGE

EARLY BRITISH PHOTOGRAPHY

themselves. We have photographs of that visit, and the Fox Talbot calotypes are fixed to a board with drawing pins; hundreds of them all around Lacock Abbey, which would make dealers weep with despair. But I don't think much got lost. The Science Museum took six thousand, we took a much smaller number, but an example of everything. Talbot didn't just invent the negative, he went on to work with something called photoglyphic engraving, from which, later on, photogravure developed. Our curator took examples of everything to show what Fox Talbot had been doing over a thirty year period. We have about three hundred images; negatives and various positives showing, for instance, how he tried to stop the photographs fading, doing everything possible to stop the yellowing of the image, or its disappearance. A lot of our Talbots are covered in a shellac varnish.

Could you still print off the original paper negatives?

Yes, it's been done. In the '60s and '70s people here did print off the originals. We now make an internegative, it's called a surrogate negative. This negative can be printed, so you don't damage the original. We have a portrait of Constance Talbot, his wife, which we think is the first portrait, from

February 1840. It's dated on the back. Before that it was inanimate objects, a lot of still life, and the famous window which is now up at the National Museum of Photography, Film and Television in Bradford. It is wonderful, a beautiful blue-brown colour. It has faded over the last hundred and fifty years. The chemicals were impure then. Silver nitrate would have other bits and pieces in it, and there are chemical reactions which are very hard to predict. Some of the material is pale yellow, others purple-blue.

So you keep a watchful eye on things?

We try, but technical monitoring can't be done

SILVER IMAGE

EARLY BRITISH PHOTOGRAPHY

with the human eye, you have to do densitometer readings to see what's happening. The originals are kept in acid free boxes, on metal shelving in a dark room, and are not often exhibited.

The Royal Photographic Society
Fenton House, 122 Wells Road, Bath BA2 3AH, England.
Telephone +44 (0)1225 462841
Research appointments only

SILVER IMAGE

EARLY BRITISH PHOTOGRAPHY

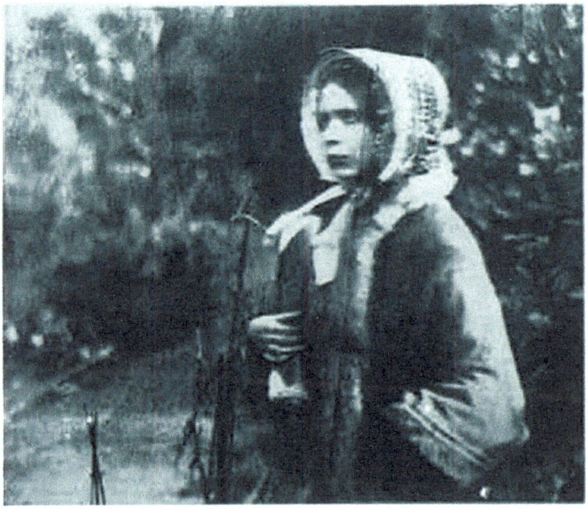

An Unknown Girl Salt print c.1843
(The daughter of The Rev.Calvert Richard Jones ?)
Cv/VAR Archive

INTERVIEWS-ARTISTS

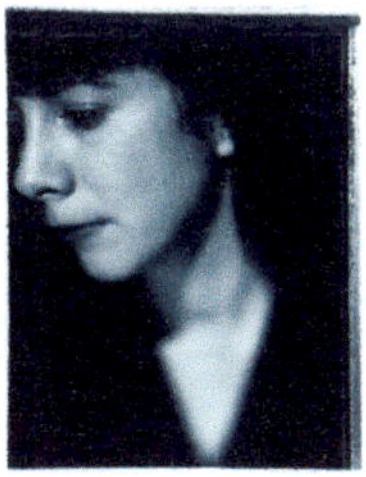

Karen Knorr Photo: Colin Jarvie
Courtesy of the Artist

Interviews-Artists: *Recordings from Cv/Visual Arts Research* ISBN 1-905571-50-X Format: A5 size (21 x 14.8 cms), softback, perfect bound. 144 pages, bw ill List price £14.99

First published in 1993 *Interviews-Artists* is a body of recorded conversations made since 1988. In considering their work, often in the context of a current exhibition, established and emerging artists from Arman and Sir Anthony Caro to James Turrell and Rachel Whiteread discuss their ideas in formation and the factors which have informed their development. Read together, another picture emerges of unexpected links between the makers, in the expression of their concerns, in the work and with the world beyond, that forms a unique and coherent overview of the developing art of our time.

Arman . Elspeth Barratt . Nicola Bealing . Denis Bowen . Stuart Brisley . Anthony Caro . Helen Chadwick . Brian Clarke . John Cobb . Lynn Dennison . Brian Eno . Garry Fabian . Julia Farrer . Rose Garrard . John Goto . David Griffiths . Leslie Hakim-Dowek . Anthea Holmes . Tam Joseph . Peter Kennard . Phillip King . John Latham . Jock McFadyen . Maurizio Nannucci . Guy Noble . Hughie O'Donoghue . Gloria Ortega . Eduardo Paolozzi . Michael Porter . June Redfern . Louise Sheridan . John Skelton . Paramjit Takhar . Gérard Titus-Carmel . James Turrell . Sheila Vollmer . Rachel Whiteread . Alison Wilding . Richard Wilson .

Contents folder at www.tracksdirectory.ision.co.uk/artists

Other titles from Cv/Visual Arts Research

CURATORS & COLLECTIONS

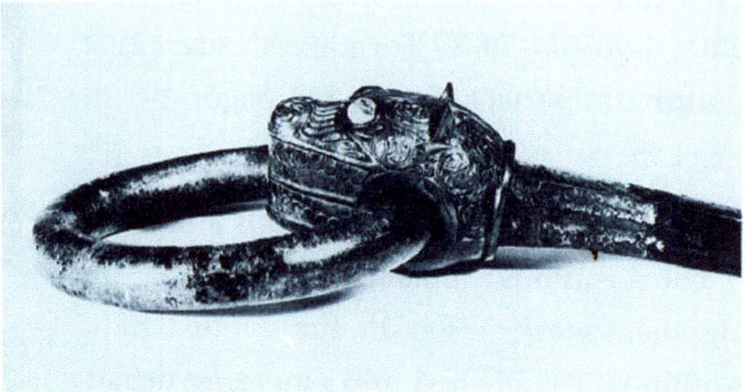

Animal Head with ring. Bronze with glass eyes. Irish 9th Century.
Collection The Nation Museum of Ireland. By permission of The British Museum

Cv: Visual Arts Research Volume 4

Curators & Collections: Conservation of the Arts Ed.James/Batiste

ISBN 1-904727-18-2

Book format: A5 size (21 x 14cms), softback, perfect bound with laminated covers.

128 pages, bw ill.. £12.99

Part 1. Curators interviews:

CENTRE DU VERRE PARIS *Jean Luc Olivie on Bohemian Glass at Musee Des Arts Decoratifs* ; COURTAULD COLLECTION *John Murdoch on Samuel Courtauld;* IMMA DUBLIN *David Rose & Declan MacGonagle* ; NATIONAL GALLERY *Early Italian Painting + Renoir & The Impressionists* ; TREASURES OF DERRYNAFLAN *Michael Ryan on Early Celtic Metalwork at The British Museum;* ROYAL PHOTOGRAPHIC SOCIETY BATH *Pamela Roberts on Collection of The RPS at Bath* ; THEATRE MUSEUM *Stage Designs and Effects at The Theatre Museum, Covent Garden* ; NATWEST ART COLLECTION Rosemary Harris; DOCUMENTA X, KASSEL *Catherine David In Conference;* TATE MODERN IN CONSTRUCTION *Dawn Austwick & Jeremy Lewison on the new Tate, Bankside*

Part 2. Collections Guide, England, Wales and Scotland.

Other titles from Cv/Visual Arts Research

Cv/VAR Software Titles November 2007 Audio CDs

ARMAN Conversations with Objects 1905571712	Cv/VAR 47 documents an interview with the French sculptor Arman, exploring his early connections with Yves Klein, Rosicricianism, and the development of auto-formed sculptures of collected objects. Contents: Van Gogh . Iris Clert . Yves Klein . Claud Pascal . Jackson Pollock . Poliakoff . De Stael . Werkmann . Garbage Works . Welded Pieces The Orchestral Series . Gods and Goddesses. . Biographical data **Wave audio file mastered from the original recording + pdf reader & A3 foldout £19.99**
HELEN CHADWICK Of Mutability 1905571720	An interview with the artist at her Beck Road studio in 1989 explores the body-actionphotographic works by Helen Chadwick (d.1996)Contents: Ego Geometria Sum . Encounters and situations . Of Mutability . Bavarian palaces . On the Roccoco . The Oval Court . Lumina . Blood Hyphen . Viral Landscapes . Biographical data. **Wave audio file mastered from the original recording + pdf reader & A3 transcript £19.99**
HUGHIE O'DONOGHUE Sleeper 190557178X	Interview recorded at his Columbia Road studio in 1989 with leading painter Hughie O'Donoghue. Source of his influences from Michelangelo and The Laöcoon in Rome to El Greco and his View of Toledo. Thoughts on the dynamic of the paintings. Comments on in-progress Sleeper Diptych and Irish Sea paintings. Contents: The Laocoon . Bacchus and Ariadne . El Greco . Abyss . Sleeper . The Irish Sea **Wave audio file mastered from the original recording + pdf reader & A3 foldout £19.99**
MICHAEL PORTER Derbyshire Woods 1905571852	Painter Michael Porter interviewed in 1990 at his studio describes favourite motifs, a foot square of the site of Ambergate Woods in Derbyshire from which he develops some richly mysterious compositions.Contents: Initial Studies . Derbyshire Woods . John Constable, Boat at the Lock and Helmingham Dell . Methods and interpretations **Wave audio file mastered from the original recording + pdf reader & A3 foldout £19.99**
JAMES TURRELL Inside Outside 190557181X	Interview with American artist James Turrell recorded in June 1996 explores work with light and major projects such as The Roden Crater environmental sculpture. Contents: The Mendota Hotel, Ocean Park . Shallow Space Constructions . Plato's Cave . Full Vision . The Roden Crater Project . Ambient Light . Soft Cell . Geologic Time . Biographical Data. **Wave audio file mastered from the original recording + pdf reader & A3 foldout £19.99**
ALISON WILDING Harbour 1905571895	Interviewed in 1996 at her Bermondsey studio sculptor Alison Wilding describes the making of Harbour, a large alabaster piece; the source of the stone, the methods of creation and the role of her assistants. Contents: Fauld Mine Staffordshire . On dissonant materials . Echo . Anya Gallacio . Adam Kershaw . **Wave audio file mastered from the original recording + pdf reader & A3 foldout £19.99**

Artists audio CD ROMs: Arman . Stuart Brisley . Anthony Caro . Helen Chadwick . John Cobb . Coffin Price . Debbie Duffin . Garry Fabian Miller . Rose Garrard . Maurizio Nannucci. Guy Noble . Hughie O'Donoghue . John Skelton . Gérard Titus-Carmel . James Turrell . Elspeth Barratt . Julia Farrer .Tam Joseph . Phillip King . John Latham . Elizabeth Magill . Eduardo Paolozzi . Michael Porter . Louise Sheridan . Rachel Whiteread . Alison Wilding

$40 by air. Card order (Visa, Mastercard) from Cv Publications Tel: +44 (0) 20 8400 6160 (Secure line)

For catalogue information of Cv titles in print contact:
Cv Publications . 10 Barley Mow Passage .
Chiswick . London . W4 4PH UK
Tel: +44(0)20 8400 6160
www.tracksdirectory.ision.co.uk